Pictorial
Map of LONDON

SCALE

0   ¼   ½   ¾   1 MILE

Railways and Stations ━━■━━
Underground Stations ●

'Crown Copyright reserved'

Acknowledgment

The publishers wish to thank J Simpkins of the London Planetarium for the picture on page 26 and the British Tourist Authority for the picture on page 27.

Popperfoto supplied photographs for the cover and pages 10, 11 (top), 12, 13, 14/15 (bottom), 16 (top), 21 (top), 38, 39.

Roger Bradley took the photographs on pages 4/5, 48, 50, 51.

© LADYBIRD BOOKS LTD MCMLXXX

Learnabout...
London

written and
photographed by
JOHN MOYES

Ladybird Books
Loughborough

London

London is the most daunting city for a stranger and yet, only a little beneath the surface, the most friendly. It is a huge sprawling city, both in size and population. London is the home of the Queen and the Royal Family. It is the seat of Government, of Justice and the centre of Finance and Investment.

You must see London on foot, not in a car (you'll never be able to park it!) If you feel tired you can hail a taxi or take one of the red buses for a short journey. The

*Waterloo bridge and the London skyline
seen from Hungerford bridge*

Underground System, which is an exciting challenge to the uninitiated, will take you quickly over longer journeys. It is more difficult to travel by public transport during 'rush hours' (between 0800 hours and 0930 hours, and 1700 hours and 1800 hours).

You can stay as long as you like in the places that interest you and not spend so long in those that don't. You can always revisit them another time.

Houses of Parliament

Go first, by bus or taxi, across Westminster Bridge to the South Bank of the River Thames and walk for a while along the Albert Embankment. From here you will have the finest view of the Houses of Parliament, or more correctly, the Palace of Westminster. The old Palace was the home of the king for several hundred years until, in 1529, King Henry VIII took Whitehall Palace, and moved to live there.

Ever since then the Palace of Westminster has housed Parliament. In 1834 it was mostly destroyed by fire and only Westminster Hall, the Crypt chapel, the Cloisters and the Jewel tower survived. The present building was designed by Sir Charles Barry, who also designed Tower Bridge. It is said to have as many windows as there are days in the year.

At the south-west corner, the Victoria Tower is the largest and tallest square tower in the world. A flag flies from this tower when Parliament is sitting. At the south-east corner is the famous clock tower, known to everyone as 'Big Ben', though this is really the name of the great bell which chimes the hour.

Walk now towards Big Ben, over Westminster Bridge, and you are leaving behind you on your right, County Hall, offices of the Greater London Council. Across the river you see Queen Boadicea (Boudicca) in her chariot.

At certain times when Parliament is not sitting, it is possible to visit the Houses of Parliament. You would then see Westminster Hall with its marvellous hammer beam roof of Sussex oak.

Westminster Abbey

Across Old Palace Yard from the Houses of Parliament is Westminster Abbey. A church has stood on this site, once called Thorney Island, since Saxon times. In the year AD 750, a Benedictine Abbey was founded here. It was known as West Monastery (West-Minster), from its position two miles west of London's centre. Edward the Confessor rebuilt it and subsequent kings have restored it, repaired it and added embellishments of their own. The most recent addition was the two graceful towers at its western end. These were designed by Nicholas Hawksmoor in 1735.

From Norman times our monarchs have been crowned there and, since the thirteenth century, it is there that they have been buried. The Abbey is not under the see of a bishop. It is administered by the Dean and Chapter and technically its status is like that of St George's Chapel at Windsor Castle, known as 'royal peculiar'.

Inside the West door is the finest view of the Abbey, and from here its immense grandeur is put into perspective. As you move on inside, past plaques and statues, there is the architectural splendour of Henry VII's Chapel and the Lady Chapel, with its amazingly intricate stonework. By contrast there is the simplicity of the tomb of Edward the Confessor, and also the Coronation Chair. In Poets' Corner you will find statues and, underfoot, the tombs of poets like T S Eliot.

Outside the Abbey, walk through Dean's Yard and into Great Smith Street on the way to Parliament Square.

Westminster Abbey viewed from Dean's Yard

Whitehall

As you cross Parliament Square from the Abbey, notice the statues surrounding it, notably the one of Sir Winston Churchill, who stands facing Parliament with as much courage and authority as he did when alive.

Walking up Parliament Street, along Whitehall, you pass through the heart of the country's government. Here, until it burned down in 1698, stood Whitehall Palace with its rose-red Tudor brick, its green lawns and shining marble statuary. Now nothing remains of all that self-indulgent splendour but the beautiful Banqueting House, designed in Palladian style by Inigo Jones. It was from one of the windows of this building that King Charles I stepped to the scaffold in 1649.

of poppies on Remembrance Day.

A short distance away is Downing Street, where the Prime Minister lives at Number 10.

Further up Whitehall, two of the Queen's Life Guards, on beautifully groomed horses, stand sentry at the entrance of Horse Guards. Try to be there before eleven o'clock (ten o'clock on Sundays) for the Changing of the Guard. This is one of the most colourful events in everyday London.

Charles I's statue was successfully hidden from Oliver Cromwell's Commonwealth Government by a brazier who had been told to melt it down. It now stands at the top of Whitehall on the site where those who condemned him were themselves executed. Behind the statue is a plaque which marks the point in London from which all distances are measured.

In the middle of Whitehall is the Cenotaph where the Queen lays the first wreath

One of the Queen's Life Guards

11

London Parks

On through the arch under the Clock Tower is the old Tilting Yard of Whitehall Palace, now called Horse Guards Parade. It is here, on the nearest Saturday to her official birthday of June 2nd, that the Queen takes the salute at the Ceremony of the Trooping of the Colour.

Stretching before you is St James's Park. There are nearly eight hundred acres of parkland in Central London. Until 1953 sheep were kept in Hyde Park and neighbouring Kensington Gardens to crop the grass.

Kensington Gardens

Horse Guards Parade seen from St James's Park

St James's Park lies between the Mall and Birdcage Walk and was redesigned by Charles II, who loved to walk there. The lake is the home of many birds. Ducks and geese waddle pompously along its banks, and you may even see a pelican. Many Londoners feed them. Try to go back one evening and stand on the bridge over the lake with floodlit fountains playing on either side, and the London skyline rising above the tree tops.

Buckingham Palace

In the distance, you may hear the sound of a Military Band. Go along to Buckingham Palace where you may see the Guards as they play themselves out of the forecourt, and march back to barracks. They are a fine sight with their scarlet tunics and the sheen of their bearskins as they march in perfect unison.

Buckingham Palace was purchased from the Duke of Buckingham by George II and was re-built in 1835 to a design by John Nash. This elegant style, now known as Regency, appears frequently in London. 'Buck House', as it has been nicknamed by Londoners, has been the home of the sovereign since Queen Victoria's reign, and the Royal Standard flies overhead whenever the Queen is in residence.

Queen Victoria Memorial

In front of the Palace is the Queen Victoria Memorial.

If you turn your back on the Palace and walk under the lime trees which border the Mall, you can turn left into Stable Yard and go to Clarence House and St James's Palace. Clarence House is the home of the Queen Mother, and it was here that, before she ascended the throne, the Queen gave birth to Princess Anne.

Clarence House

changed: a small but impressive ceremony.

Around the north-west corner of the Palace, Cleveland Row joins Pall Mall and St James's Street. Here are the homes of Gentlemen's (and nowadays Ladies') Clubs. Here you are on the southern border of the West End. Walk up St James's Street and you will see fine old shops where gentlemen have bought shoes, hats and wine for over two hundred years.

St James's Palace and the West End

St James's Palace became a home for the Royal Family when Whitehall Palace was destroyed in 1698. At the eastern end of the courtyard is the Chapel Royal which has a beautiful painted ceiling attributed to Holbein. Here the choristers still wear a Tudor uniform of scarlet and gold. Shortly after one o'clock you will see the sentries being

Lock and Co. in St James's Street

17

Continue up St James's Street and turn right into Piccadilly. On the northern side of Piccadilly is Burlington House, home of the Royal Academy of Arts. Ahead of you is Piccadilly Circus itself, the hub of London's West End and the heart of Theatreland. The graceful curve of Regent Street is on your left, Shaftesbury Avenue and Leicester Square lie ahead. You should revisit Piccadilly Circus at night when the statue of Eros is given some rest from constant traffic driving round. Now move on down Haymarket to Trafalgar Square.

The Post Office Tower
A modern landmark
compared with the
old shops in St James's Street

Wine merchants in St James's Street, Berry Bros. and Rudd.
Famous for Port and Claret

Trafalgar Square

Trafalgar Square was laid out early in the last century to commemorate Admiral Lord Nelson's last victory at the Battle of Trafalgar. Nelson stands heroically on his column overlooking Whitehall, with Admiralty Arch and the Admiralty at his feet. Everything happens here, from the discord of protest marches, to the harmony of carol singing round the huge Christmas tree sent to Britain by Norway every year. Nelson is guarded by four stone lions designed by Edwin Landseer.

However, it is not the lions that dominate Trafalgar Square, but the pigeons. If you buy some grain from the vendors to feed them, they will walk along your arm and even perch on your head.

Admiralty Arch

Behind Nelson is the National Gallery, in which you will find paintings by Rubens, Rembrandt, Constable, Turner and many others. At the north-east corner of the square is the beautiful church of St Martin-in-the-Fields. James Gibbs was the architect, and the vicars of St Martin's have a special tradition of care for the poor and needy in the true spirit of Christianity.

The National Gallery

In Duncannon Street, by St Martin's, you can find a bus to take you along the Strand. At either end of the crescent of the Aldwych, are two of London's prettiest churches, St Mary-le-Strand, also by James Gibbs, and St Clement Danes by Christopher Wren. It is the latter church you will remember from the children's rhyme "Oranges and Lemons say the bells of St Clement's."

Church of St Mary-le-Strand

21

The Law Courts and the British Museum

At the end of the Strand, the castellated building that faces you, with its romantic turrets and sugar-loaf towers, is the Law Courts, seat of Civil Legislature. This marks the eastern border of London's West End and beyond this lies Fleet Street, the centre of the newspaper world, and the City. Cross the road now and cut through Clement's Inn to Portsmouth Street where you will find a 16th century antique shop that claims to be the original of Charles Dickens' 'Old Curiosity Shop'.

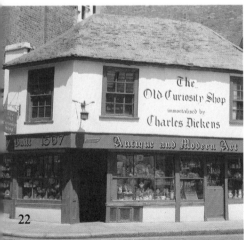

As you walk on into Kingsway, it is a short walk, or a shorter taxi ride, to the British Museum. Nowhere else in the world will you find such a collection of treasures gathered together under the same roof.

The Law Courts

London contains many other museums which you may visit on another day. At South Kensington, easily reached by Underground, are the Victoria and Albert Museum, and the Natural History and Science Museums. In the Science Museum you will find almost every aspect of scientific evolution, from James Watt's original Beam Engine, to Atomic Power. Stephenson's 'Rocket' is there, as is 'Puffing Billy', and there are many working models which start at the press of a button.

The British Museum

More Museums and Exhibitions

The Natural History Museum with its terracotta slabs, tall towers and Romanesque portico is typical of the Victorian architecture found around London. The museum has a fine collection of minerals, meteorites and precious stones as well as examples of every animal, fish, bird and mammal that has ever existed. The huge skeleton of a dinosaur is the collection's pride, as is the life-size model of the Blue Whale.

The Natural History Museum

You should also try to find time to visit the Museum of London in the Barbican near St Paul's. This museum covers over 2000 years of the history of London.

Madame Tussaud's

Next door to Baker Street Station is the Waxworks Exhibition of Madame Tussaud's. Here you can rub shoulders with the famous, not only from the pages of history books, but also from the worlds

of Politics and Art, Sport and Entertainment. Minute attention has been given to detail, both of the figures themselves and their costume; one mass murderer who appears in the Chamber of Horrors actually sent his suit to Madame Tussaud's the day before his execution. You will be amazed at how small were some of the powerful people of the past! You can also walk through the lower decks of *H.M.S. Victory* during the Battle of Trafalgar and see the gunners as they would have been during the action.

The Planetarium

In the Planetarium you can sit back in your seat while all the stars of the Northern Hemisphere move across the simulated night sky above you. A superb commentary will recreate for you the superstitious fears and beliefs of your ancestors and speculate on the predictions of astronomers for years to come.

The City *The Lord Mayor's coach passing the Law Courts*

The City of London, once a walled fortress, occupies an area of only one square mile. It is full of tradition and you may see it better on a Sunday, so avoiding the busy week-day traffic. The City is the heart of the Nation's Commerce and the titles of its Guilds or Livery Companies reflect the businesses conducted as early as the 14th century; the Mercer's Company, the Haberdashers, the Goldsmiths, the Fishmongers.

The City is governed by its own Corporation headed by the Lord Mayor. A new Lord Mayor is elected each year, and each November he rides in his elaborate coach, made in 1756, through the streets of the City. After this journey he travels to the Law Courts where he is received by the Queen's representative, the Lord Chief Justice. In the evening, at the Guildhall, he and his Sheriffs give a banquet at which they entertain the Prime Minister and members of the Government.

Of all Christopher Wren's churches, the City is dominated by St Paul's Cathedral made of white Portland stone, in warm contrast to the masculinity of the City.

Once inside, above you is the dome, second in size only to St Peter's in Rome. In reality this is two domes. The inner is of brick and the outer of timber sheathed with lead. Between the two is a brick-built cone which supports the 700 tons weight of the Golden Gallery and the gilded ball and cross above it. You may climb up to the 'Whispering Gallery' (where a whisper really can be heard the other side) and even into the ball itself. The height from the top of the cross to the pavement is 365 feet, one foot for each day of the year.

In the Clock Tower is the largest bell in England, Great Paul, which is rung for five minutes every day and was cast in Loughborough, Leicestershire.

After a short walk down Prince's Street you are in the City's centre. It is from the steps of the Royal Exchange (picture below) that a new monarch is proclaimed. Ahead and to the left is the Mansion House (picture right) which is the official residence of the Lord Mayor. This contains, among other treasures, a beautiful 8,000-piece chandelier of Waterford glass. On your right is the Bank of England, (picture far right) also nicknamed 'Old Lady of Threadneedle Street.'

Down King William Street is the Monument, erected in 1677, to commemorate the Great Fire which broke out in a baker's shop in Pudding Lane only a few yards away. It is possible to climb the 311 steps to the top of the Monument, but the view is now obscured by many high-rise office blocks.

After the Great Fire, Christopher Wren the architect
began to rebuild the City. The Monument was partly his,
together with three exquisite churches; St Stephen's
Walbrook, St Margaret Pattens and St Mary-Le-Bow.
The last is known all over the world, for a true Cockney
must be born within a mile of 'Bow' bells. The air-raids
of the last war made way for the Barbican development
which will be the London home of the Royal
Shakespeare Company and also provide housing within
the City.

Little Venice and the Zoological Gardens

Though you can travel to the Zoo by bus or taxi, a more pleasant way is by boat. Near Warwick

Avenue Underground Station, the British Waterways Board have dredged and landscaped the junction of the Grand Union and Regent's Canals to make a pool, overlooked by pretty houses. This is known as Little Venice. Here you may board a Narrow Boat (it is incorrect to call it a Canal Barge) which will take you along the Regent's Canal to the Zoo. It's a fascinating journey and gives a glimpse of the importance of our canal system in the last century.

At the Zoo, children may ride a camel, or the very young be pulled in a cart by a llama. You should

also see the sea-lions being fed. With such a wide variety of animals in a lovely setting, the Zoo will give you an afternoon to remember.

Chessington Zoo

Half-an-hour's ride on a train from Waterloo Station will bring you to Chessington Zoo. This is a family Zoo, with something for everyone. Apart from the animals, there is a boating lake, a circus, a fair-ground and a miniature train which will take you right through the grounds. A new addition, well worth seeing, is 'the World of Mechanical Music', which is an extraordinary collection of unusual musical instruments.

There is a choice of Restaurants and Snack Bars, and a Model Village, but of course most important are the animals and the birds, especially the penguins who have their own ornamental lake.

London's River

Wordsworth wrote:
"This City now doth, like
a garment wear
The beauty of the morning;
silent bare,
Ships, towers, domes,
theatres and temples lie
Open unto the fields
and to the sky;
All bright and glittering
in the smokeless air."

You must go down to the river and see all these things for yourself. There are many waterbuses and river launches, and you may take one to Greenwich and have lunch on board on the way.

Without the river, London would never have been built. Though diminished now as a port, London can be proud of the River Thames. Work by the water authorities over the past twenty years has transformed it from a turgid, stinking sewer to a home once more for bass, sea-trout, and even salmon.

You can take the waterbus from Charing Cross pier by the Embankment Underground Station, on a delightful journey to the Tower of London. On the left is Cleopatra's Needle and across the river is the Royal Festival Hall. Through Waterloo Bridge, on your right, you will see the new National Theatre. The photograph above shows four permanently moored ships. HMS *Discovery*, was originally the Polar research vessel which, in 1901, took Captain Scott to the Antarctic. The *Wellington* is now the Livery Hall of the Honourable

Company of Master Mariners, and the *Chrysanthemum* and the *President* are training ships for the Royal Naval Volunteer Reserve. HMS *Discovery* has since been moved to St Katherine's Dock, where it is part of the Maritime Trust Collection. Beyond Blackfriar's Bridge there is another fine view of St Paul's; it was in a house on the South Bank that Sir Christopher Wren lived during the cathedral's construction.

The National Theatre

Down River to the Tower

On down to London Bridge where there stood, until 1749, London's only bridge. Then houses, shops, and even a church stood on the bridge itself. On the South Bank is the beautiful Gothic, Southwark Cathedral where William Shakespeare used to worship. Passing under the bridge you come to the Pool of London, where HMS *Belfast*, heroine of the Second World War, lies at her moorings. She is now a naval museum.

Tower Bridge, with its two decorated towers, has twin drawbridges, each weighing 1,000 tons, both operated by hydraulic power. As you disembark at the Tower of London, you should notice Traitor's Gate, now bricked up.

Tower Bridge

The Tower of London

It was William the Conqueror, nine hundred years ago, who first built a fortress here. The White Tower, built of white Caen stone from Normandy in France, is the nucleus of the Tower of London. Later kings added to it. It has served as a palace as well as a fortress, but it is as a prison that it is known best.

The road of Royal Succession was a bumpy one, and not always was the throne of England secure and uncontested. Often England was ruled well and justly, but there were times when excessive zeal, greed and stupidity filled the Tower with political prisoners. Three queens were beheaded at the Tower, two princes are supposed to have been murdered, and the screams of the tortured are still said to haunt the dungeons.

You will see the Yeoman Warders in their Tudor uniforms. They are often mis-called 'Beefeaters'. Also in the Tower are the Crown Jewels, heavily guarded. Only once, in Charles II's reign, were they stolen, and the thief got no further than Traitor's Gate. The surprising outcome of his trial was that he was awarded a pension for life, as it was whispered that the King himself had instigated the robbery.

The White Tower contains a fine collection of arms and armour, and the Beauchamp Tower, with initials carved in the stone,

tells of noble prisoners of long ago. The ravens on Tower Green are the last remnants of the Royal menagerie of Henry VIII. There is a superstition that should the ravens leave the Tower of London, Britain and the Commonwealth will crumble. Today the ravens' wings are kept severely clipped!

From the Tower, you can walk past the cannons and under Tower Bridge to St Katherine's Dock where there is now a modern Yacht Marina. *Discovery* to be seen here amongst other ships, is part of the Maritime Trust Collection.

A hundred years ago the river was full of sailing barges, going to and from the docks with cargoes of imported goods for the little shallow harbours of the Thames Estuary. Now there are only about twenty sailing barges but you may be lucky enough to see a Barge race, which is quite a spectacle!

41

Down River to Greenwich

At Tower pier you can take a launch down-tide. A delightful commentary will tell you of riverside history and you will see for yourself the wharfs and taverns where past dark deeds were done. Through Wapping and Limehouse, Bermondsey and Rotherhithe you will come to the Isle of Dogs where King Charles kept his famous spaniels. At the southern tip of the Isle is a small park called Island Garden. From here there is a fine view of Greenwich waterfront on the other side of the river. As it approaches Greenwich Pier, the launch will make a wide turn. This will give you the best view of the Royal Naval College which was built on the site where

The Royal Naval College

Greenwich Palace once stood. Henry VIII was born at Greenwich Palace and so were his daughters, Mary and Elizabeth.

In 1694, Sir Christopher Wren designed the Royal Hospital for Seamen in the Classical style. It was this building which became the Royal Naval College in 1873. The College is open most afternoons and inside you will see Wren's Painted Hall and Chapel. Also note the marvellous ceilings painted in the Baroque style by James Thornhill. Admiral Lord Nelson had his lying in state in the hall before he was buried in St Paul's Cathedral.

Greenwich

At the head of Greenwich Pier is the champion
tea clipper, 'Cutty Sark,' which dwarfs the little 'Gipsy
Moth IV' in which, in 1966-67 Sir Francis Chichester
sailed single-handed round the world. You can visit both
of these.

Look at the Queen's House, home of the National
Maritime Museum. This was designed by Inigo Jones for
the wife of James I in 1617. The East and West wings of
this elegant white-stone building were not added until
1807. This was the first example of the Palladian style to
appear in England, and is flanked on either side by
magnificent colonnades. The exhibition is in

The Queen's House

chronological order and starts in the Queen's House in Tudor times when Henry VIII founded the Royal Navy. With models, paintings, relics and actual ships, the museum traces the evolution of ships and seamanship up to the present day.

In Greenwich Park you may climb the hill to Flamsteed House, the original site of the Royal Observatory. Standing on the Zero Meridian of Longitude, you will enjoy one of London's finest views. You could then return from Greenwich by train instead of by launch.

Hampton Court Palace

You can travel all the way to Hampton Court Palace by water, but it's a long journey. You would be better to go by train from Waterloo. The Palace has a fascinating history. Like Whitehall Palace, it was built for Cardinal Wolsey, and when he fell from the King's favour, Henry VIII took both palaces for his own. Here he hunted deer and courted the ladies who were to become his wives.

At this time all of Europe was trying to rebuild in the style of the Palace of Versailles. Hampton Court was saved from this fate by a shortage of funds. Instead, William and Mary settled for renovation, and employed Sir Christopher Wren. In consequence, Hampton Court, set in graceful gardens and bordered by the Thames, embodies some of the very best of British architecture. You can walk through its State Rooms and Royal

24-hour clock at Hampton Court Palace

Apartments which have been beautifully preserved. Here also are the portraits of the ladies of the Court of Charles II. All these paintings were by Sir Peter Lely.

Outside in the orangery, you will see the two hundred year old vine and perhaps lose yourself in the famous Hampton Court maze.

Hampton Court remained the favourite Palace of monarchs until, in the middle of the eighteenth century, George III moved to the quietness of Kew so that he could concentrate on his Colonial Policy.

By River to Kew Gardens

From just outside
Hampton Court Palace it's
a leisurely journey by
launch, through trees and
parkland, down to Kew.
Through Teddington Lock
you will be in the tideway,
soon through Ham and
Richmond, and in Kew.
From here it is a short
walk to Kew Gardens.

The Royal Botanical
Gardens are the home of
serious scientific research.

Plants of all kinds are grown there, and from studies of them, botanists have been able to recommend what kind of wheat should be grown in Canada, and what plant will yield the most rubber in Malaysia. But this is not just a research station. In Kew you will find flower beds and parkland and perhaps have a picnic by the Pagoda. The Plant House is like a hot, South American jungle.

London at night

In London in the evening there is the finest selection of entertainment to be found anywhere in the world. There is Opera and Ballet (for which you must book well in advance) and at the Theatre, your choice is unlimited. A spectacular musical is only across the road from a Shakespeare season or a knock-about farce. You may see, in the flesh, the actors who, through film and television, have become household names.

Young people will find numerous discos, and there is also jazz. There is the Summer Season of Promenade Concerts (known as the 'Proms') at the Royal Albert Hall. Over the river, at the Royal Festival Hall you will find the widest possible range of programmes, international orchestras, conductors and soloists. Acoustically, this is one of the finest Concert Halls in the world.

After the concert, stand where you began your tour of London in this book, on the banks of the Thames, and see the lights of the Victoria Embankment reflected in the river. Cross to Waterloo Bridge and you will see St Paul's, flood-lit.

Whenever you visit London, whether your stay is a long one or even if you only have a short time, everyone is assured of something to wonder at, something which will entertain or just a memory to take away from this fascinating city.